A New True Book

GREAT SMOKY MOUNTAINS

NATIONAL PARK

By David Petersen

CHILDRENS PRESS®

CHICAGO

John Oliver Place, Cades Cove, in
Great Smoky Mountains National Park

Project Editor: Fran Dyra
Design: Margrit Fiddle

Library of Congress Cataloging-in-Publication Data

Petersen, David.
  Great Smoky Mountains National Park / by David
Petersen.
      p.   cm. — (A New true book)
  Includes index.
  ISBN 0-516-01332-7
  1. Great Smoky Mountains National Park (N.C. and
Tenn.)—Juvenile literature.   2.   Natural history—
Great Smoky Mountains National Park (N.C. and
Tenn.)—Juvenile literature.   I.   Title.
F443.G7P47   1993
976.8'89—dc20   92-35049
                                                    CIP
                                                    AC

TABLE OF CONTENTS

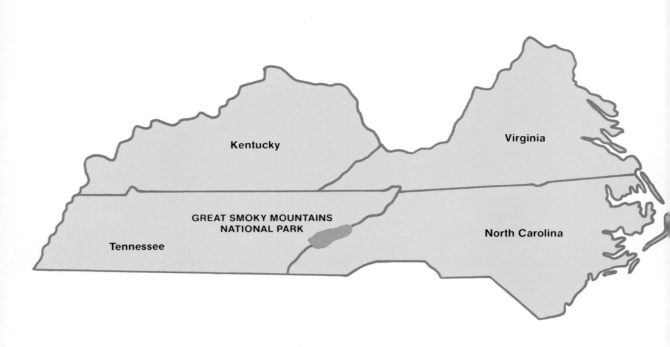

Kentucky

Virginia

Tennessee

GREAT SMOKY MOUNTAINS
NATIONAL PARK

North Carolina

This view of Newfound Gap shows the blue haze
that gives the Great Smokies their name.

A WILDERNESS TREASURE

Great Smoky Mountains National Park is a half-million acres of wilderness, wildlife, and history. After the Florida Everglades, it is the largest natural area in the eastern United States.

The park lies half in Tennessee and half in North Carolina.

NATURAL HISTORY

The mountains that give the park its name—the Great Smokies—are part of a larger range called the Appalachians. The Appalachian Mountains extend from Canada on the north down to Georgia and Alabama in the south.

CANADA

APPALACHIAN MOUNTAINS

The flat-bottomed mountain valleys in the Smokies are called coves.

The Appalachians and the Smokies are very old mountains. Millions of years ago, pressures deep in the Earth pushed them up. Since then, wind, water, and other forces of erosion have rounded and worn down the mountains.

LAND OF THE CHEROKEE

For thousands of years, the Smokies belonged to the Cherokee people. The Cherokee lived in large permanent villages. They hunted, fished, gathered wild foods, and raised gardens.

Then, in the late 1700s, European settlers began to arrive. For years, the settlers and the Cherokee lived side by side. But more and more settlers came, and they all wanted land.

THE TRAIL OF TEARS

Oklahoma

- - - - Land route
—— Water route

Finally, in the 1830s, the Cherokee were forced to leave the Smokies. Soldiers marched them hundreds of miles to Indian Territory, now called Oklahoma. Many Cherokee died on this "Trail of Tears."

9

At the Museum of the Cherokee Indian (far left) and the Oconaluftee Indian Village (above), the Cherokee honor the arts and crafts of their ancestors. The woman at left works beads into traditional designs.

But a few Cherokee hid from the soldiers and never left the Smokies. Today, their descendants live on the Cherokee Reservation next to the park. Many natural features

An 18th-century Cherokee home at Oconaluftee Village (left).
A Cherokee woman decorates pottery (right).

and towns in the Smoky Mountains have Cherokee names. In fact, the name Smoky Mountains itself comes from a Cherokee word, *Shagonigei,* which means "blue smoke place." This is a good

Forests cover almost all of the Great Smoky Mountains.

name because the Great Smokies are almost always blanketed with a blue, smoky haze. This haze forms because tons of water vapor and natural plant oils are released into the air by the forests.

SETTLEMENT

As soon as the settlers arrived in the Smokies, they began cutting down trees. The settlers needed lots of open land to raise crops and livestock. Corn was the most important crop. Horses, cows, pigs, chickens, geese, and bees were the most common farm animals.

Preserved buildings from pioneer times: the Elijah Oliver cabin (above) and the Missionary Baptist Church (inset) in Cades Cove

The settlers also cut trees to get logs. They made strong buildings from the logs. Dozens of these old log buildings are preserved in the park today. There are houses, churches, barns, mills, and one-room schools.

At the Oconaluftee Farmstead, you can visit a historic farmhouse and barn. And you can wander among live farm animals.

Mingus grain mill (left) and the farmhouse at Oconaluftee Farmstead (above)

In the Oconaluftee house (left) meals were cooked over an open fire.
The Mingus mill (right) ground grain for local farmers.

At Cades Cove and at the Farmstead, local mountain people use historic buildings as "living museums." There they demonstrate the skills of their pioneer ancestors—cooking over an open fire, weaving, and grain milling.

Along with farming, the pioneers hunted and gathered wild edible plants—just as the Native Americans had done before them. In the beginning, the Smokies were full of deer, bears, turkeys, and other wild animals. But over the years, hunters killed off most of the wildlife.

The forests, too, were abused. The Native Americans and the early settlers had always cut

The early settlers cut down trees to clear land for crops (above). Later, lumber companies cut so many trees that the forests were destroyed.

trees only for their own needs. But in the 1900s, timber became a valuable product. Companies moved into the Smokies, and millions of trees were cut down. By the 1930s, about 70 percent of the area had been stripped of its

18

John D. Rockefeller
(1839-1937)

trees. The bare mountains were ugly, and wildlife had no place to live.

A few wise people began working to save what remained of the forests and wildlife. They wanted to make the area into a park.

A wealthy man named John D. Rockefeller contributed $5 million to buy land for the park. The states of Tennessee and North Carolina each contributed $2 million. The rest came from thousands of small gifts. Schoolchildren helped as well, collecting nickels and dimes.

In 1934, Great Smoky Mountains National Park was born. From that time on, no logging or hunting was allowed. Today, much of the land once stripped

In the forests of the Smokies (left), you can see birds such as the mockingbird (top right) and the Tennessee warbler (above).

bare by loggers is again covered with trees. And many of the birds and animals have returned.

21

WILDLIFE

The Great Smoky Mountains are home to more than 60 species of mammals and more than 200 kinds of birds. The best times of day to see wildlife are at sunset and sunrise. This is when wild animals come out of hiding to eat and drink.

The best place to see park wildlife is around Cades Cove. Look for wild turkeys and deer where

Animals such as the white-tailed buck and fawn (top left), turkeys (left), and black bears (above) live in the Smokies.

woods meet fields. If you're lucky, you might even see a bear!

The black bear is the Smokies' largest animal. Biologists believe about 400 black bears live in the park.

The forests of the Smokies are home to small animals such as the skunk (left) and the red squirrel (right).

The park animals are used to people. Some of them seem almost tame. But it's a mistake to feed or pet them. Bears are dangerous because they're so big. And even small animals—like squirrels and skunks—can bite and carry diseases.

Deer feed on meadow grasses in the early morning mist.

FORESTS

There is so much wildlife in the park because the habitat provides them with food, water, and places to hide. Good habitat includes meadows, streams, and lots of trees. More than 100 kinds of trees grow in the forests of the Great Smoky Mountains.

Hemlocks grow along streams and in other low areas. The hemlock is an evergreen tree. Evergreens have long, narrow needles instead of broad leaves. And as their name suggests, evergreens keep their green needles the year around.

Opposite page: Hemlocks and rhododendrons by a mountain stream

Cove hardwoods (left) in spring,
a tulip poplar (top right), in summer,
and oak leaves in the fall (bottom right)

A little higher up grow
the cove hardwoods. These
include broad-leaved trees like
poplars, oaks, and maples.
Hardwoods grow new
leaves each spring, and
drop them each fall. One
place to see these big

Newfound Gap

trees is along the Cove
Hardwoods Nature Trail, off
Newfound Gap Road.

Northern hardwoods live
a little higher yet. Two of
the most common are beech
and birch. Newfound Gap
is one of the best places
to see these trees.

29

In the fall, the forests of the Smokies glow with red, yellow, and orange leaves.

Fall is the most colorful time of year to visit the hardwood forests. Each October, thousands of people come to the Smokies to watch the millions of hardwood leaves turn from green to brilliant yellows and golds.

The highest mountaintops, such as Clingmans Dome, are covered by forests of spruce and fir trees. Like their hemlock cousins down in the valleys, spruce and fir trees are evergreens.

Clingmans Dome Observation Deck in the Great Smoky Mountains

WILDFLOWERS

Wood sorrel

Another beautiful season to visit the Smokies is late spring and early summer. This is when the park's 1,500 species of flowering plants are in bloom.

Wildflowers cover the ground. One lovely wildflower is the snowy white wood sorrel, with its candy-striped cups.

Mountain laurel (left) and azalea (right) in bloom

Flowers also bloom on
shrubs called heaths.
Among the prettiest of
heath flowers are the
flame azalea, rhododendron,
and mountain laurel. And
one of the best places
to see heaths is on balds.   **33**

BALDS

Balds are mysterious clearings in the mountain forests. Most are on mountaintops. Some balds

Rhododendrons bloom on a bald in the Smokies.

are covered with heaths. Others have only grass. Exactly what causes these bald spots in the woods is a mystery. But they are great places to visit. Andrews Bald is the easiest to reach. It's a two-mile hike from the Clingmans Dome parking area, along the Forney Ridge Trail.

HIKING

The park has many hiking trails. The shortest and easiest trails are called Quiet Walkways.

"Self-guiding nature trails" are longer walks. For each of these trails, there is a booklet describing plants and other interesting things you will see along the way.

You can learn even more on the ranger-guided hikes. But if you want a

A hiker enjoys a spectacular mountaintop view.

real adventure, strap on a backpack and hike into the park's backcountry. There, you can wander almost forever.

In all, there are almost 900 miles of trails in Great Smoky Mountains National Park.

WATERFALLS

Some of the park trails lead to rushing waterfalls. A waterfall is a place where a stream falls over the edge of a cliff into a pool below. Waterfalls can be big or small. There are several big waterfalls in the park. Some can be seen from roads, but most require some hiking to reach.

Laurel Falls is one of many beautiful waterfalls in the Smokies.

CAMPING

Camping is another outdoor adventure you can find in the Smokies. Many park campgrounds can be reached by car. They have toilets, drinking water, fireplaces, and picnic tables. But some of the park's

People enjoy picnics in the park.

Beautiful scenery and historic buildings attract visitors
to Great Smoky Mountains National Park.

best campgrounds can be
reached only by walking
or riding horses. These
walk-in campgrounds have
no facilities. But they are
far less crowded, quieter,
and more natural than the
roadside camps.

FISHING

While hiking and camping, you may want to try fishing. The clear, cold streams of the Smokies are home to three kinds of trout. Trout are beautiful

Little River is one of the many great fishing streams in the Smokies.

Rainbow
trout

fish–fun to catch and
delicious to eat. Rainbow
and German brown trout
are plentiful.

The third kind of trout in
the park is the native
brook trout. The "brookie"
is a protected species in
the Smokies. It must be
gently returned to the
water if caught.

TOURING BY CAR

Of course, not all visitors to Great Smoky Mountains National Park hike, camp, or fish. In fact, many people see the park only from their cars. Along the 270 miles

A highway in the forest near Newfound Gap

Grotto Falls (right) and changing leaves in early fall

of park roads, you can
see forests, wildflowers,
historic buildings, streams,
waterfalls, and wildlife.

But the best parts of *all*
national parks are found
beyond the roads. That's
where nature lives undisturbed. **45**

WORDS YOU SHOULD KNOW

abused (uh • BYOOZED) — treated badly; not used wisely or well

ancestor (AN • ses • ter) — a grandparent or forebear earlier in history

Appalachians (ap • ah • LAY • shins) — a mountain range in the eastern United States

azalea (uh • ZAYL • yuh) — a shrub with large, colorful flowers

bald (BAWLD) — a mountain patch of ground where there are no trees

biologist (by • AHL • uh • gist) — a scientist who studies living things

cove (COHV) — in the Smokies, a flat-bottomed mountain valley

demonstrate (DEH • mun • strayt) — to show how to do something

descendants (dih • SEN • dintz) — a child or a grandchild; a person who comes later in a family line

edible (EH • dih • bil) — able to be eaten

erosion (ih • ROE • jun) — the wearing away of the land by wind, water, or ice

evergreens (EV • er • greenz) — trees having small, needlelike leaves that stay green all year

habitat (HAB • ih • tat) — the place where an animal lives

hardwood (HARD • wood) — trees that grow broad leaves in the spring and drop them in the fall

heath (HEETH) — a name for some kinds of wild shrubs that grow in the Smokies

hemlock (HEM • lock) — an evergreen tree

historic (hiss • TOR • ick) — like something in the past

laurel (LAW • ril) — a heath shrub with clusters of small flowers

livestock (LYVE • stahk) — animals kept by farmers, such as cows and pigs

mammal (MAM • il) — one of a group of warm-blooded animals that have hair and nurse their young with milk

permanent (PER • muh • nint) — lasting a long time

pioneer (pye • uh • NEER) — one of the first settlers in an area

preserved (prih • ZERVD) — kept as it was in the past

rhododendron (roh • duh • DEN • drun) — a heath shrub with large, showy flowers

settlers (SET • lerz) — people who come to a new area to live and work

Shagonigei (Shah • go • nee • GAY • ee) — a Cherokee word meaning "blue smoke place"

species (SPEE • ceez) — a group of plants or animals that are of the same kind

timber (TIM • ber) — trees that are to be cut down and made into wood for people to use

trout (TROUT) — a fish found in lakes and streams that is good to eat

water vapor (WAW • ter VAY • per) — water that has been turned into a gas by heating

wilderness (WIL • der • niss) — a natural area without towns or farms

INDEX

About the Author

David Petersen is a nature writer living in Colorado. He formerly lived in North Carolina near Great Smoky Mountains National Park and visited there often.